THE BIG CELL

Children in the Bible

Andy and Catherine Kennedy

Authentic
LIFESTYLE

SPRING
HARVEST
Equipping the Church for action

First published 2003 by Spring Harvest Publishing Division and Authentic Lifestyle.

07 06 05 04 03   7 6 5 4 3 2 1
Authentic Lifestyle is a division of Authentic Media,
9 Holdom Avenue, Bletchley, Milton Keynes, Bucks, MK1 1QR, UK.

British Library Cataloguing in Publication Data
A catalogue record for this book is available from the British Library

1-85078-513-9

Cover and text design by Giles Davies Design
Illustrations by Giles Davies
Printed in Great Britain by Bell and Bain Ltd, Glasgow

CONTENTS

Check This Out Kids!

What is 'The Big Cell'?

It's ten weeks of material designed especially for children aged 8–12, to help them lead their own cells.

What is a Cell?

A cell is a small group of about 3–7 children, who get together to pray for their friends and the world, have fun, explore the Bible, listen to God and get to know Him better. Jesus said that 'if two or three people come together in my name, I am there with them.' (Matthew 18:20)

Wow! So cell is a place where you can expect to meet Jesus.

Here are five important things a cell should aim for:

1 Jesus at the centre
2 Care and Belonging
3 Everyone with a part to play
4 Servant leadership
5 Prayer

How Do Cell Sessions Work?

They work using Four Ws:

Welcome – time for fun together
Worship – time to focus on God and tell Him how great He is
Word – time to explore the Bible
Work it Out – time to pray and get practical.

You will see these 'Four Ws' as you read through this book. We recommend you share out the Ws so a different member of the cell leads each one. You could change the leaders every week!

We also suggest a fifth W – **a Wise Person** – an adult who helps the cell. They might be in the room with you when you meet, they might be in the next room or nearby. If you decide to start a cell, you need to decide as a group who your Wise Person is going to be. They might be one of your parents, a children's leader in your church, or some one else who knows Jesus well. Ask this person to pray about being your adult supporter who you can go to with questions, problems, prayer needs and so on.

How Long Does a Cell Session Last?

Every session is designed to last an hour. Each W has the number of minutes it should take written underneath. The sessions could of course last longer or shorter depending on how much you pray, talk etc!

Getting Started...

When will you meet? Talk to your friends, put some dates in your diaries. We suggest you find a time and stick to it each week. It could be at school during lunchtime, after school in one of your homes or a Sunday afternoon. We already know of one cell where they meet for breakfast each Sunday. Make sure you all check out the time you choose with your family – they may have things planned!

What Cell is Not...

Cell is not a replacement for what you do at church with your leaders. You need to pray for your leaders and find ways to encourage them through what you do in cell.

It is not a gang that makes other people feel left out. You need to be careful about this right from the beginning, and get advice from your Wise Person if you think there may be a chance of this.

Check This Out Grown Ups!

What is 'The Big Cell'?

'The Big Cell' is material specifically designed for children aged 8–12 to use in peer-led cells, with the help and advice of a wise adult.

Peer-led Children's Cells?

Isn't That a Bit Dangerous?

The Big Cell recognises that leadership ability is evident in young people even before they hit adolescence and their teen years. Many children in our churches are so well fed that they are 'fed up'. Few, however, are really given the chance to exercise the gifts God has given them, to take a lead and to rely on God in new ways. Cells are one way in which children can take on leadership and responsibility in 'bite-sized chunks' with the covering and support of their 'Wise Person'.

Does this fit my situation?

You may have a group of children who you know are ready for this challenge. You may have a group who still need an adult's supervision, but are ready to be given a chance to lead. You may just be looking for new material to use with your children's group! There is no reason why this material could not be used in any of these circumstances, whether led by children or adults.

Who is the 'Wise Person'?

The structure of each session is based on four Ws – 'Welcome', 'Worship', 'Word' and 'Work it Out'. These aspects are explained further in the *Check This Out Kids!* page.

We have added a fifth W – the 'Wise Person'. This is the mature adult who fulfils an important role in the cell through supporting and guiding the children without taking control in any way. They would not necessarily need to be present during cell sessions – in fact, this might inhibit some children! A Wise Person may be in the next room or a phone call away. Their role is to help the children prepare, to answer questions, to provide debrief after sessions and to help sort out any problems arising. Above all, they should lovingly and prayerfully encourage the children in their quest to know God better.

One idea to consider is to organise a short meeting of all parents and children to share the vision and values of 'The Big Cell'. It would be an excellent start for the children to have their parents pray for them.

The Big Cell Web Site:

www.kingskidsengland.co.uk

You may be interested to know that there is a Web site where children's cells can connect with each other, find out what God is doing among them across the nation and get fresh ideas and inspiration. Children must make sure they do this with their parent's knowledge and agreement. Why not log in together as a whole cell along with the Wise Person?

'The Big Cell' is a ministry of King's Kids England. King's Kids is a part of Youth With A Mission.

5

Things to help your Cell times

Be Prepared!

This material is laid out so that you as a cell group can divide the responsibilities up for the session. If you agree to lead one of the W sections for a cell group do not turn up at cell group expecting it all to just happen.

It is very important to be prepared in advance. This material will only work if you get your props and equipment ahead of time.

Treat your part seriously and pray about it. Do it for God first and foremost. If you have problems in your preparation, then give another member of the cell a call, or call the Wise Person.

The Worship Wall

A Worship Wall is a great thing to have for your cell group worship time. You could make one very easily with some card and paint, and use it in all sorts of ways. It could be a place to:

● Stick prayers of thanks and praise to God
● Bring things you want to offer back to God
● Stick worship poems
● Place models and pictures you have created in worship

Your group will probably think of loads more ideas!

See page 43 for more instructions, and signs to photocopy.

The Journal

A Journal is like a diary that you can write in every week as part of Cell. The 'Work it Out' section usually has an activity for you to do in your Journal.

It's great to be able to look back and see what you were thinking about and praying for, especially when you see God answering your prayers.

You can use all sorts of things as a Journal:

● A Notebook
● A Diary
● A Scrapbook
● Lots of pieces of paper stapled together!

Why not cover your Journal with funky paper, and put your cell group's name on it (as well as your own). You could design a logo on the computer. Why not meet as a group and all have fun doing it together!

You will know it's time to use your Journal when you see the words:

Journal Time

Remember to bring your Journal to cell group every time you meet.

Other helpful things to have:

● Bibles
● A CD or cassette player
● Worship CDs and cassettes e.g. Jim Bailey *Children of the Cross*; Doug Horley *Woopah Wahey*; Spring Harvest Kids albums; Ishmael *52 Scripture Songs*; H_2O *A Gift from the Father*. Matt Redman, Tim Hughes or Delirious are excellent too!
● Pens (for Journal Time)

Look out for special items you will need for each session.

1 How God sees children

YOU WILL NEED

A4 paper
felt-tip pens
sellotape

Encourage-mental!

Stick a piece of A4 paper to everyone's back. Each person is given a felt-tip pen. Put music on in the background. The idea is for everyone to move around the cell and write encouraging things about everyone else on their pieces of paper. After 5 minutes each person takes the paper on their back and reads it.

5 minutes

YOU WILL NEED

CD/cassette player
CD/cassette
plasticine

Worship sculptures

► Put on a CD/cassette worship song, e.g. *Colours of Salvation* by Jim Bailey or *Forever* on the H$_2$O album.

► As you listen to it, make shapes, sculptures and patterns with plasticine which are inspired by what you hear.

► You could even sing along as you do it! Display your models at the Worship Wall.

10 minutes

word

Over the next few weeks the cell is going to look at stories of children and young people in the Bible. We will discover as we read that God thinks very highly of children. He sees them as able to believe in Him; worship Him; be filled with His Spirit; pray to Him; meet angels, be used by Him in incredible ways to perform miracles; care for others; be humble and willing; face very difficult and dangerous situations and walk in amazing faith and obedience.

To do

Between you as a group try to think of any places in the Bible where children or young people are mentioned. What lessons can we learn?

Now read

Use the following Bible references to discover more.

Psalm 8:2

These are young children! The Hebrew word is ol'al and it means children still being breast fed by mum. Wow, that's young isn't it!

Exodus 31:1–5

Bazelel was reckoned to be 13 years old by ancient Jewish tradition. Look what happened when he was filled with the Spirit of God!

Joel 2:28

This part of the Old Testament is quoted by Peter on the Day of Pentecost when he preached to a large crowd (see Acts 2). This Old Testament verse began to be fulfilled as the church was born on the Day of Pentecost, but we're still waiting to see God's Spirit poured out on the whole world. When you think that half of the people in the world are under the age of 16, then the Lord wants to pour out His Holy Spirit on children everywhere. Wow, that's exciting news!

20 minutes

After reading Joel why not ask God to do this for you as a cell group.

Read 1 Timothy 4:12

Journal Time

▶ Look at the list mentioned and ask yourself what area(s) you feel weak in. Write what you are thinking in your journal.

▶ Tell each other and pray for each other, asking for God's help.

20 minutes

Remember to speak to your Wise Person and let him/her know how you got on today with the first cell time.

Did you know?

▶ The Big Cell is part of the King's Kids ministry of YWAM.

▶ If your cell would like to hear from other cells in the country and share what God is doing, then you can apply for a user password and become part of Big Cell on-line.

▶ Check out www.kingskidsengland.co.uk for more details.

2 Jesus – a special journey

Hide 'n' Seek game

The cell leader gets to hide sweets around the house you are meeting in. The rest are then asked to go find them. Don't eat them until you return so everyone can share!

5 minutes

YOU WILL NEED

sweets

Balloon Praise!

Write lots of things you are thankful to God for on small bits of paper. Just use 1 or 2 words on each piece.

- Roll them up to fit down the neck of each balloon. Inflate the balloons and tie knots in them.

- Put on a favourite music track and throw all the balloons in the air. Try and keep them up without any of them hitting the floor!

- When the music stops (somebody needs to decide when) each person grabs one balloon. Burst them, but don't lose the pieces of paper.

- Now everybody speaks out the things that were written down.

7 minutes

YOU WILL NEED

balloons
pens and paper
CD/cassette player
a favourite CD/ cassette

In the Bible we don't hear much about Jesus during his growing up years. We know a lot about his birth and celebrate it each year at Christmas. In Luke Chapter 2, we see him at 8 days old when he's presented at the Temple, which was normally done with baby boys at the time. Matthew Chapter 2 tells us how he has to escape to Egypt. He's probably around 2 years old. He grows up in Egypt until it's safe to return after Herod dies. When they do return, the family settle in Nazareth, in the far north of Israel. Nazareth is Jesus' home for most of his life. We next meet Jesus when he is 12 years old, and here's the story...

Find out what happened next

Read this together:

Luke 2:41–52

Some questions to ask

▶ We know Jesus never sinned or did anything wrong in His life, that's why He was able to die for us. So what do you think about what happened here? He goes missing for 3 or 4 days with no explanations to his mum or dad!

▶ How do you see God? Do you see him as your dad? It's obvious that something very special happened to Jesus on this trip to Jerusalem for the festival. When they did at last find him, his parents were astonished to find him in the Temple. They were particularly astonished when he said to them 'You should have known that I must be where my Father's work is!'

▶ At the end of the chapter we read how Jesus continues to grow up and that he is obedient to his parents. Obedience is not a very popular word today!

▶ What about you in the cell group? Be honest! Are you obedient to your parents? Is it easy or hard for you? Is there any advice you can give to each other? Look up Ephesians 6:1–4. If Jesus did it, it must be important! What do you think?

30 minutes

In Luke 2 we see Jesus, a 12-year-old boy, asking and answering questions with the religious leaders in the Temple. As a cell group, what 5 questions would you really like to ask your Church Leaders or Wise Person? It could be about anything really e.g. hard questions about God or how they see children in their church...

Think of the 5 questions now.

1 _____

2 _____

3 _____

4 _____

5 _____

10 minutes

Your Wise Person could help you arrange a time to meet up with a church leader. Why not call them now.

Meet up on the Web

Please ask permission first.
We'd love to know your hard questions too and also hear some of the answers you get. Why not tell us on the Web site! Have a great week...

Web Site: www.kingskidsengland.co.uk

Next cell session

Be ready for the worship section next time. Find something that is important to you. It could be your football, Play Station, CDs, a poster of a popstar, a magazine you read, a ring... or whatever is valuable to you. Bring it along to the next cell meeting.

13

3 Daniel – the young man who didn't follow the crowd

YOU WILL NEED

paper and pen

Angels and Mortals

Here is an activity that lasts for a week until you next meet as a cell. Everyone puts a piece of paper with their name on into a hat or box. Now each person takes a piece of paper (if you get your own name put it back). The aim of this game is to be an angel to each other without them knowing it's you. It's all meant to be secret! Pass on encouraging little notes or gifts or get someone else (even your teacher!) to do something for them. Be creative with your ideas, and we dare you to do it in school too!

`all week!`

worship

YOU WILL NEED

Worship wall

CD/cassettes

CD/cassette player

What's important?

You will need to think about this activity before you meet together. Tell the cell the week before and phone around to remind everyone. Find something that is important to you. It could be your football, Play Station, your CDs, a poster of a pop star, a magazine you read, your ring... or whatever is valuable to you! Bring it along when you meet and be ready to place it at the Worship Wall.

► Play a couple of songs on the CD that you like and as the music plays each person quietly and slowly places the object they brought at the Worship Wall.

► When the song has finished each person prays out loud a prayer like 'Lord, I give you this football. Thanks for sports and fun like football, but I just want to say Lord that you are more important to me than this.'

► Put up the words 'Be true' on the Worship Wall.

`10 minutes`

word

Background *Read this out loud:*

The powerful King of Babylon, Nebuchadnezzar, had come and captured Israel. He asked for some of the bright young guys from Israel to be trained in his language and customs so that after a while they could serve him in his court. Daniel and his three friends were picked for this task. However, Daniel was worried because all the young men were expected to eat food from the King's own table – this food was cooked in a way that didn't follow God's law...

Dreams were considered very important at that time. The book of Daniel has a few of them.

Find out what happened next

Take it in turns to read a few lines from this amazing story.
Look up these verses (yes, the whole story!).

Daniel 1:8–21; 3:1–30

Some questions to ask

▶ These young guys learned to respond to their difficult situations by getting together and praying (Chapter 2:17–18). Do you think they were a kind of a cell group and what can you learn from them?

▶ Can you think of anyone else in the Bible who had dreams which came true? How else did dreams play a part in his life?

25 minutes

Develop good habits

Daniel and his three friends had a good habit in their lives – they regularly prayed on their own and with each other. Standing together as a cell to help each other is the most important thing about being a cell.

Creative prayer idea

Circle Trust

► Take it in turns to stand in the middle of the group with everyone else standing around them in a circle. The person in the middle puts their hands by their side, keeps their feet together and closes their eyes. The others GENTLY push them from one side to the other. No talking allowed as it is more powerful if it is done quietly. It is VERY IMPORTANT not to let the person fall. The idea is to make them feel supported by the rest and that each person in the cell can trust the others.

► After each person has had their turn, pray for that person for a minute in the circle.

10 minutes

WISE PERSON

Go and ask your Wise Person if you can pray for them this week. Do they have a particular prayer need?

This week

► Don't forget to do 'Angels and Mortals' this week and keep it a secret. Get your school friends involved.

► Why not telephone or email each other this week at least once to ask what to pray for...

4 Esther – born for such a time as this

True or False

Each cell group member gets a piece of paper and a pen. Write down 3 things about yourself. Make two of them true but one false. Now go around around the group reading out your three things. Everyone has to guess which ones are false.

12 minutes

YOU WILL NEED

paper and pens

You're not a mistake!

► Put the music on and be still and quiet for 1–2 minutes to focus yourselves.

35,783, 35,784, 35,785, 35,786, 35,787...

► Read Psalm 139 together. Why not take a few lines each. Don't force people to read though. Especially concentrate on verses 13–16. In fact, why not try to memorise them for next week's cell group.

► Put up the phrase 'You're not a mistake!' on the Worship Wall.

8 minutes

YOU WILL NEED

CD/cassette of instrumental music (no words!)

CD/cassette player

4
4

word

Background *Read this out loud:*

Esther, an orphan, and her cousin Mordecai, were Jews who had been captured and taken to live in a foreign land. The King of that land, Xerxes, fell out with his wife, sent her packing and ordered that many girls from his kingdom be brought to his palace to see if he liked any of them better! Esther was one of these girls. Xerxes thought she was gorgeous, and made her his Queen.

Up until this point, the story could be a bit like Cinderella – however there was a bad guy in this tale. Haman was a nobleman, and the King had made him higher than all the other noblemen. Haman was extremely proud of himself for this and expected everyone to bow down to him. Mordecai, Esther's cousin, would not do so. Haman discovered that Mordecai was a Jew and hatched an evil plot to get rid of all the Jews – anyone who killed a Jew would be paid a lot of money. Mordecai got wind of Haman's evil plan and went out into the city, weeping and wailing...

Find out what happened next

Esther 4:4–17

Some questions to ask

▶ What situations have you been in where you knew you had to speak out or stand up for someone/something, but you also knew it could be dangerous or cause you problems? Share your stories with each other...

▶ Mordecai believed (see v.14) that Esther was not in her position as Queen by mistake. What does this story tell you about how God can use young people?

15 minutes

4

18

4

Journal Time

▶ Despite being a captured slave girl, Esther had many gifts and abilities from God which helped her when she was Queen.
In your journal, write down three gifts/talents God has given you.

▶ God has created you for a special purpose, just like Queen Esther. Take time now to think and pray about this. How does God want to use you to make a difference? Look at the gifts and talents you wrote down – they are a good place to start.

▶ Write down in your personal journal one situation God wants you to make a difference in. It could be the school sports team, if you're good at sport. It might be in befriending shy kids if you love talking to people.

20 minutes

Get in touch with your Wise Person soon and let him/her know what God is teaching you as a cell group.

5 Samuel – a boy who heard God speak

Blind Corners

Blindfold everyone in the cell group except the leader of the activity. One large piece of string or rope is given to the group. Tell the group they have 2 minutes to make a perfect square with the string. People are allowed to speak to each other, but not to peek! The leader watches and observes to see how they do it.

After 2 minutes, ask the team to remove their blindfolds to see how well they have done the task. What did the group learn or feel when they were doing it? Was it hard? Did they argue or did they listen to each other? Did someone take the lead or did everyone try to become the leader?

YOU WILL NEED

blindfolds for all except one of the group

a long piece of string

5 minutes

We're listening!

The Psalms were actually songs with music.
Read Psalm 8 together to give you an idea of one.

▶ Take 10 minutes now to write your own poem or song to God. Tell Him what is on your mind. If you can make a tune to go with it then all the better.

▶ After 10 minutes share back what you have written, even if you feel it isn't finished yet.

Some of you will have written really nice prayers and words. If there wasn't enough time in cell group why not decide to finish what you have begun at home and add a tune to share for next cell group.

▶ Put up the words 'We're listening' on the Worship Wall.

YOU WILL NEED

paper and pens

20 minutes

Background *Read this out loud:*

Samuel was the son of Hannah, a lady who thought she would never have children. When she gave birth to Samuel she was so grateful that she gave him back to God by sending him to serve in the Temple. Eli the priest looked after him and taught him. People wonder how old Samuel was when the events of this story happened. The word used for him is the Hebrew word 'Naar'. This means 'shaking free' and is used for young people around 10–13 years old, an age Jews see as the crossover time between childhood and adulthood.

Find out what happened next

Read these verses together

1 Samuel 3:1–21

Some questions to ask

▶ Why do you think God spoke to Samuel out loud?

▶ Why do you think He chose Samuel to tell such an important message?

▶ When he grew up, Samuel became known as a prophet – he spoke out what God was saying. God started to treat Samuel as a prophet when he was still a young boy. Does this tell you anything about God?

15 minutes

Practise makes perfect!

Samuel was not used to hearing God's voice – he didn't know it was God speaking to him at first. We need to practice hearing God's voice too.

5 Steps

Here are 5 simple steps in preparing to hear God speak. Use them together as a cell, and invite God to come and speak to each of you.

Be Thankful

The Bible tells us that a good way to come into God's presence is with thanks ('Come into His city with songs of thaksgiving...thank Him, and praise his name' Psalm 100:4). Say thank you to God for who He is and what He's done for you. Everyone pray, using one or two words only, 'machine-gun' style (no gaps, just quick-fire prayer). See if you can do it and keep it going for a minute.

Be Sorry

Psalm 24:4 says we need to have 'clean hands and pure heart' to be in God's presence. Quietly, on your own, ask the Holy Spirit to come and shine like a torch into your life, showing up the things that don't please Him. If He shows you something, say sorry and ask for forgiveness. If He shows you something you need to make right with another person in the room, go and do it. Be radical! If the person is not in your cell, then agree with the Lord that you will speak to that person as soon as you can. You may even have to make a telephone call. Jesus' teaching is clear – we are forgiven as we forgive others.

Be Filled

Stand in a circle. Put your hand on the shoulder of the person to your left. Ask one member of the cell to say a prayer asking God to fill each person in the cell with His Holy Spirit. Thank God that He has given us the Helper (another name for the Holy Spirit) to help us hear from God and pray to Him.

Be Quiet

Ask another member of the group to pray out a prayer like this 'Lord we choose to shut out any distractions from our own thoughts, and we silence the voice of the Enemy in Your Name. Lord, we choose to listen to Your voice now, and trust in your ability to speak to us'.

Be Ready and Listen

Eli taught Samuel to say 'Speak Lord. I am your servant and I am listening'. Why not have each person say this out loud in turn around the circle. Then get comfortable and ask God quietly, on your own, 'How, or in what ways have I brought joy to your heart this week?'

► After listening for a few minutes, get into small groups of two or three and share with each other what you felt God saying to you. If you didn't feel you heard anything, don't worry. It takes practice to learn to hear from God in this way – look how many times it took Samuel! So don't give up.

12 minutes

Journal Time

► Why not write down what you've just talked about in your journal?

5 minutes

★ Key Idea

Learning to hear from God is a very important thing for any cell to do. God has lots to share with the people who take time to listen. One secret is to ask God specific questions, such as, 'God, how do you see or feel about our city?' Or they could be asking God about how He sees your school or asking God for guidance in decisions/choices you have to make.

WISE PERSON

As the cell gets good at hearing from God it is very important for you to share what you feel God is saying to you as a group with your Wise Person.

6 A refugee girl who came to the rescue

welcome

Sticky Situation

Every person in the cell gets a similar-sized piece of sellotape. Now, all at the same time, put it above your top lip, just under your nose. The leader says 'Go!' and the winner is the person who manages to wriggle or shake free the sellotape first. No hands allowed! Repeat once or twice.

5 minutes

worship

Clean Up!

Please ask an adult for advice.

▶ Here is a cool worship idea for today's cell. If you are meeting in a home then take 10/15 minutes as a cell group to help with a practical chore or job around the house. Bless mum out of her socks!

▶ If you are meeting in a school then is there something you could do to help, e.g. with litter or sweeping up?

▶ If someone has written a song from last week's cell then this is the time to share it.

▶ Put up the word 'Healing' on the Worship Wall.

20 minutes

In Israel it was a time of lots of fighting and war. There was a famous man called Elisha alive at the time whom God used in very special ways to try and turn the people back to God's ways, and back to the worship of the one true God.

Today's story is about a girl who, although we don't know her name or anything much about her, was ready and willing for God to use her. Outwardly she didn't exactly have it all going for her. Think about this: she'd lost her family, been taken prisoner and made into a refugee. Then, as a refugee, she'd been made a slave! How would you feel?

Find out what happened next

Read these verses together (If you would like to find out what happened to Naaman, then read the whole chapter!)

2 Kings 5:1–6

Some questions to ask

No questions today – just go straight to Work It Out.

15 minutes

You need help with that!

Journal Time

► Think of people you know who are sick or unwell. Write their names into your journal.

► In what practical ways could your cell group encourage or help them? Could you go and visit someone? Or offer to do some shopping or clear the garden? What about going to pray for someone who is sick? Even a homemade card might cheer them up!

► Decide together who you are going to bless, and make a plan of what you are going to do for them right now.

► The girl in the story went to speak to an adult who could help, in this case, the wife of Naaman himself.

20 minutes

Perhaps your Wise Person could help you. Call them now!

7 The boy who fed a hungry crowd

Here are two ideas to do with food. Choose one.

Break the ice

The idea is for the cell members to decorate 1 or 2 biscuits each! Decide on a theme like 'God is Good!' or 'Unity' or 'Light'.

When you are finished enjoy looking at each other's biscuits and eating them together with a drink.

YOU WILL NEED

Rich Tea biscuits/
Digestive biscuits

icing
(4/5 colours)

The Sweet Game

YOU WILL NEED

A selection of
sweets

Put some different types of sweets on a plate. Take it in turns to leave the room. The rest of the group decide which sweet is the 'poisoned sweet'. The person returns and starts to eat the sweets until they pick up the 'poisoned' one. If they do, then they have to stop and someone else has a turn. Carry on until all the sweets have been eaten or until everyone has had a turn.

15 minutes

worship

Going without

Sometimes people choose to go without something, maybe food or TV or anything else that's important to them. It's called 'fasting'. It can help us focus on God and show Him that we're serious about listening to Him and helping others. Many people in our world will go without today and go to bed tonight hungry.

▶ Decide how as a cell this week you can go without coke or chocolate bars and make a special donation of the money you would have spent on them to help others.

▶ Draw a picture of the thing you have decided to give up this week and stick it to the Worship Wall.

Your Wise Person or a teacher at school will know a worthwhile place to give your money. Discuss as a team when you could each 'fast' this next week. When will you collect the money in?

▶ After talking about it, pray to the Lord thanking Him that He cares for the poor and needy, and that we are so fortunate ourselves to have food.

▶ Put up the word 'miracles' on the Worship Wall.

15 minutes

word

Background *Read this out loud:*

Jesus had been healing sick people, raising the dead and drawing crowds wherever he went. On this occasion, his disciples had just come back from their own preaching and healing trips, and Jesus was getting them together in a town called Bethsaida to check out how it had gone for them. However, the local people had found out that they were in the area...

Find out what happened next

Read these verses together

John 6:1–13

Some questions to ask

▶ What did the boy have to do to see the miracle happen?

▶ Imagine being the boy who had the packed lunch...he must have had an amazing view of what Jesus did with his dinner! How do you think he felt when he saw Jesus do that with his meal?

▶ This whole miracle seems to have been planned out by Jesus (look at verse 6) so that he could test and teach the disciples as well as feed the hungry crowd. What do you think he wanted to teach them?

12 minutes

work it out

How much of a giver are you?

Sometimes we can think that what we have to offer is too small, and not good enough. The boy in the story could easily have thought:

'What's the point? My food is never going to feed this lot; I'll just keep it for myself!'

We can forget that when we give what we have to Jesus, he can use us in amazing ways. God wants us to be giving people, so that he can touch others through us.

Have a go at the quiz on the next page and find out how generous you are!

Quiz

Make sure everyone has a copy of these questions and a pen. Get each person to circle or tick the answer they choose and then add up your scores to see what you're like.

1 **When you're at school do you tend to**

a. Offer to lend people your equipment
b. Let them borrow if they ask
c. Lend things only to your friends
d. Only use your equipment yourself

2 **When someone on your table is stuck with work do you**

a. Always help them out
b. Help them if the teacher's busy
c. Help them if they're going to get told off
d. Hope someone else will help them

3 **If your brother or sister wanted to borrow a CD of yours, would you**

a. Lend it to them and not think about it till they gave it back
b. Lend it to them with a time limit
c. Lend it to them if it was a CD you weren't that bothered about
d. say 'Hands off my CD!'

4 **It gets to the end of a meal time. Would you**

a. Offer to do the washing up
b. Do the washing up because it's your turn on the rota
c. Do the washing up if you're asked
d. Never do the washing up at home

5 **Your friend really needs £5 more to be able to afford the new PlayStation game they've saved up for. Would you**

a. Give it to them
b. Give it to them if you can use the game too
c. Lend them the money, and they can pay back later
d. Let them wait till they've saved up enough

Add up your scores

A = 6
B = 4
C = 2
D = 0

25–30 You are a fantastic giver who gives without expecting to get back. Keep it up, you generous person!

16–24 You are often thoughtful in giving people your time, help and possessions. Why not challenge yourself to look out for more opportunities to give?

8–15 You usually give when it's not going to cost you too much! Why not take up the challenge to give when you wouldn't usually do so? Look for opportunities this week.

0–7 You don't like giving, do you! Or maybe you don't see where your giving is needed. Why not go and talk to your Wise Person about it.

▶ Finish your cell group time by praying for 2/3 friends each at school. Ask the Lord for ways you can show his kindness by being a good friend to them.

15 minutes

Don't forget to talk to your Wise Person about how to give away the money you will collect this week.

8 Mary – a girl who was willing and ready

Baby Photo Fun

Ask everyone in the cell ahead of time to bring in a baby photo of themselves. Mix them up because the fun begins when we have to match each person to the baby!

You can also develop this game by using baby pictures of your parents, teachers, Wise Person.

8 minutes

YOU WILL NEED

baby photos

It's my favourite!

▶ Two or three people need to be ready to share their favourite verses from the Bible and read them out. Tell everyone why you like them.

▶ Or choose one of your favourite worship songs and say 'why' you like it.

▶ Put up the words 'willing' and 'ready' onto the Worship Wall.

12 minutes

YOU WILL NEED

2 or 3 people ready to share

Girls in Mary's time were usually promised in marriage at around 13 or 14 years of age. Mary would have been around this age when the angel Gabriel came to her with a life-changing message – that she was going to have a baby! Her cousin Elizabeth was also expecting a baby. The same angel told Elizabeth's husband about it. His reaction as an older person was very different to Mary's (if you want to read about him then check Luke 1: 5–25).

Find out what happened next

Read this together

Luke 1:26–45

Some questions to ask

▶ How did Mary first react to the angel? Why do you think she felt like that?

▶ What did Mary say just before the angel left her (v.38)? What had Mary decided?

▶ God had given Mary a very important job, which she was probably scared about for some time. How do you think she felt when she heard what her cousin Elizabeth had to say?

20 minutes

Who-me?!

Are you obedient to God?

Mary was ready to do what God asked her to do. She was obedient and trusted Him even when she was afraid. It wasn't an easy decision – she was going to have to live through some tough times, being pregnant when she wasn't married.

▶ Is there an area in your life where you find it really hard to be obedient to God? It could be
- when you're with your school mates
- how you use your time
- how you control your temper
- how you relate to your mum and dad
- something else

▶ Let each member of the cell share an area that they struggle with in being obedient to God. (We all have them!)

Journal Time

Take a couple of minutes to write down what you struggle with as a letter to God in your journal – tell Him about how hard it is. Ask Him to help you say 'Yes' to Him when you are dealing with it in your everyday life this week.

Remember, when we are obedient and say 'Yes!' to God, we allow Him to do His best in our lives. Look at what He was able to do because Mary said 'Yes!'

20 minutes

Talk to your Wise Person about one thing that has stuck in your mind from cell this week.

9 David – the worshipping warrior

welcome

Movie Clip Challenge

One person in the cell gets to show everyone their favourite video clip from their favourite film (make sure you time it beforehand so that you don't watch too much).

They must also prepare 10 questions based on the film clip or other general knowledge questions on the film.

▶ Play the movie clip, asking the cell to watch carefully as you will be asking them questions on what they have seen.

▶ Stop the movie and ask the questions. You could either put the cell into teams or everyone could compete on their own.

12 minutes

Give it Your Best Shot!

▶ Place the cans on a chair or table, being careful not to put them near breakable objects!

▶ Players take it in turns to see if they can knock down all the cans.

8 minutes

worship

YOU WILL NEED

CD player
song tracks ready

Worship warriors

Put on Jim Bailey's CD *Children of the Cross* and play the title track. Get the group to either sing along if they know it, or else simply listen to the music. Close your eyes. Be relaxed.

At the end of the song why not continue by praying together with whatever comes into your heart and mind after listening to the song.

Put up the word 'Warrior' on the Worship Wall.

10 minutes

36

Background *Read this out loud:*

David is one of the most famous people in the Bible. He's one of the characters who we see through his whole life – from boyhood to his death. God said of him that 'he is a man after God's own heart!' Wow... and he wasn't perfect either! He made big mistakes that cost people their lives.

We first meet David as a young boy who's got 7 big brothers. How would you like that? We'll read today how God chose him instead of these brothers to be the next King. Then we'll see him fighting a giant named Goliath!

How old was he when all this was happening? Well, the Hebrew word used to describe David here is 'naar'. It actually means 'shaking free' and is often used for a boy or girl who is about 10–13. Perhaps David is 12–14 in this story.

Find out what happened next

Read together 2 whole Chapters from the Bible today!
Take it in turns to read chunks out loud.

1 Samuel 16–17

Some questions to ask

▶ As a boy, David was responsible for looking after the family's sheep (perhaps even the sheep of the whole village). He had to learn to trust God, and ask Him for the strength to do the job well. How responsible are you? Are you trustworthy, honest, reliable?

▶ What jobs are you each given to do in your families? Could you do them better? Are there jobs in your family/home that you could offer to do this week?

20 minutes

David was a worshipper from a very young age. He was the one who wrote the famous song in Psalm 23.

Prayer sword

► Everyone has a piece of card each and draws on it the shape of a sword.

► Choose one verse from Psalm 23 and write it on the 'blade'.

► Cut it out and keep this bit of God's word with you this week. God's word is powerful like a sword when we believe it and put it into practice (see Ephesians 6:17).

Use your verse as you pray this week e.g., if you chose 'I will fear no evil for you are with me' v.4, then you could pray 'Thank you Lord for being with me. Help me to trust you when I feel afraid.'

Memory challenge

Why not read Psalm 23 as a closing prayer for cell today. Keep it with you all this week.

In fact your homework this week is to memorise Psalm 23 for next Cell.

10 minutes

Show your prayer swords to your Wise Person and tell them what you are using them for this week.

10 The children were shouting out loud

Make me smile!

One person in the cell stands in the middle of the group. What they have to do is make and hold a sad or angry face while everyone else tries to make them smile, but no tickling or touching the person! When the person breaks into a smile or chuckle then it is someone elses turn.

10 minutes

●●●

YOU WILL NEED

CD/cassette player
CD/cassette

Shouting praise

Today we will meet children in the Bible who were so excited to be with Jesus that they shouted their praise out loud.

Shouting is an important part of worship. We will all know the word 'Hallelujah'. Often we say it very nicely and properly! But it is actually a Hebrew word that means to go crazy; to go mad before God because He is worthy of it!

► Why not get hold of the song 'Undignified' by Matt Redman and use it in cell today.

► After the song shout together as a group 'Jesus is the best!' 3 times. Now what else can you all shout out together about God? Go on... be brave and bold!

► Put up the word 'Shouting' on the Worship Wall.

10 minutes

word

A few weeks ago we met Jesus at 12 years old in the Temple. Here he is in the same place. He's not happy with what he sees. He is actually angry too! It's a week before Jesus is going to die. He has just surprised many people, especially some of his closest friends and disciples, by riding into the capital city of Israel, Jerusalem, on a young donkey. They had wanted a white war horse, a stallion, because they thought Jesus should use the moment to proclaim Himself King. It might have been the ideal time (Jerusalem was very busy because of a special festival taking place) to unite the nation and overthrow the Romans.

But Jesus is King of a different Kingdom. He enters Jerusalem humbly on a donkey. (This was important as it fulfilled one of the prophecies about the Messiah). As He came down the steep slope from the Mount of Olives, He would have got an excellent view of Jerusalem; the huge walls, the Temple rising straight ahead and off to His left a little. Many people join in and start shouting about who Jesus is. It affects the whole city.

The mood changes at this point in the story as Jesus enters the temple and is mad at what people have done to it. It's become like a supermarket but selling religious things. People are cheating and stealing. They've forgotten why they're there in the first place – to pray and worship.

Look who's followed Him in from the crowd – the children, the blind and the disabled. See what happens. Look at the reaction of the religious people...

Find out what happened next

Read Matt 21:1–17

Some questions to ask

▶ What did the children shout out in verse 15? Where did they get the idea to shout this out (see verse 9)?

▶ Does anyone know the meaning of the word 'Hosanna'? (It means 'Save us!')

▶ They say that children, and especially young children, are natural copycats. Perhaps you have young brothers and sisters who follow you around. Do they copy you?

▶ Who do you really look up to and admire. You might say a pop star but it must be someone who you know! What good things would you like to copy from their lives?

20 minutes

The new temple

What was the Temple in the Bible? Well...it was the place that God could live, close to his people. But it didn't work because people didn't obey God. Jesus came from Heaven to make a new way for people to live close to him, not in a building like a Temple but in people's own hearts and lives. It means that we are the Temple now for God to live in.

▶ **Church is people not a building**
Church is people who have God living inside them.
Cells are small groups where Jesus can be very real.

▶ **A place of welcome and healing**
Jesus wanted the Temple to be where children could be welcome, the sick healed and where people could call out to God to save them. 'Hosanna!' meant 'God! Save us!'

Prayer Shape

▶ Make your cell into a shape of a cell or body.

▶ Pray together asking God to help your Church be a place like that more and more.

▶ Ask God for more cells to grow that can be a safe place for children or adults too.

20 minutes

PERSON

Get together with your Wise Person for a meeting to talk about how these 10 sesions have gone.

- What have you learned from being part of a cell?
- What has God shown you through studying the lives of children in the Bible?
- What were the highlights of the last 10 sessions?
- Did you have any difficulties?
- Do you still want to be a cell? If so, what will you do differently? What will you keep the same?

If you have enjoyed these 10 sessions, there is another Big Cell book you could use next time called *History Makers*.

Instructions to make your Worship wall

1 This worship wall needs to be prepared in advance. It is easily transportable if made from cardboard. It can either lean against a wall, or if folded, it will free stand.

2 Decorate it in some way so it is attractive. We painted ours white with ready mixed paint available from any art store. Allow the paint to dry and sponge-print 'bricks' using a large sponge, to imitate a brick wall pattern. You could either do red or brown bricks. When this is dry, we painted the words 'worship wall' along the bottom in a graffiti style. You could buy brick patterned wallpaper or draw and paint any shapes you wish.

3 Photocopy the four 'W's: WELCOME, WORSHIP, WORD and WORK IT OUT

4 Each week attach them to the worship wall as you use them with blu tac. You could mount the four W's or laminate them if you wish.

43

welcome

d p

i

T

h

U

s

J

O

r

w

M

45

p d t o r o w E

work it out. Thought it.